EXPERIENCING GOD IN DAILY LIFE

THE HABIT OF REFLECTING ON LOVE, JOY, NEED, FEAR, SORROW, AND ANGER

**In Celebration of
the 500th Anniversary of the Birth
of St. Ignatius Loyola
1491-1991**

D1252911

Robert Fabing, S.J.

EPOCH UNIVERSAL PUBLICATIONS

IMPRIMI POTEST: John Clark, S.J. Provincial
California Province of The Society of Jesus

Cover Illustration: Michael Tang, S.J.
Back and White Prints: Michael Tang, S.J.

Printed in the United States of America
ISBN-0-915903-15-6

Second Printing

TABLE OF CONTENTS

FOREWORD

In its essential direction, this book wrote itself. In the process of considering the subject, experiencing God in daily life, one surprise after another occurred as the book seemed to me to be taking on a life of its own. The process told me what direction to take. This work was an adventure and a joy to write.

My hope in this book is to expose the riches of the prayer exercise, the examination of consciousness, in a way that would result in the reception of the intended grace: To see God in all things, in all human experience. This is a gift whose meaning is our flowering into who we have always wanted to be. It is a gift, readily given to us by the One who created us, that allows our coming to the fullness of our creative being. It remains for us to ask, to search, and to knock.

I have attempted in this book to use nonsexist language as much as possible while, at the same time, doing no harm to the flow of the English language. I have referred to the First Person of the Trinity as "Father" because of the biblical roots in Jesus and centuries-old Christian usage. I view God, however, as encompassing all of the richness of both male and female.

I would like to thank the many Jesuit spiritual directors I have had over the years who have passed on to me this habit of reflecting and so many friends whose questions to me have nurtured this "way."

Robert Fabing, S.J.
Los Altos, California

So I say to you:
"Ask, and it will be given to you;
search and you will find;
knock and the door will be
opened to you."

Luke 11:9

Chapter One

A Way to Experience God in Daily Life

The Examination of Consciousness

Experiencing God in daily life is the central task, challenge, and meaning of our lives. To seek God in daily life is to seek the very meaning of our lives. To see and to find God, the love of God, is the heart of our call, the very heart and core of our being. The task of this book, then, is to explore a method of finding God, a method of discovering God in our daily life experiences of love, joy, need, fear, sorrow, and anger. I will begin with an expose of a way or method of finding God, of discovering God. This way, this method is the examination of consciousness. Then I will apply this method of finding and discovering God to our daily life experiences of love, joy, need, fear, sorrow, and anger. My hope in this book is to afford a way of praying that will result in receiving the grace of findding God in all of the experiences of daily life.

We begin this consideration with the central feature and characteristic hallmark of the spirituality of Saint Ignatius Loyola, the sixteenth century Basque founder of the Jesuits, the Society of Jesus. The central feature and characteristic hallmark of Ignatius' spirituality is "to see God in all things", to be able to perceive the presence of God in every moment of life, every occurrence, every experience, every dynamic, every relationship we have. This is not a small gift. It is a grace and, essentially, it is for this grace, this gift, this ability, this charism, and the accompanying method of attaining it, that Ignatius was canonized a saint. Ignatius has been called a practical, down-to-earth mystic because of his undeviating desire for God. And it is this desire that brought him to seek and find God in all things.

Early in Ignatius' conversion process, he realized a need to write down in a notebook his experiences with God in prayer. He did this because he found his experiences with God to be precious, but elusive. Writing his experiences down tended to clarify their meanings. He also found that writing down his experiences with God recreated the experiences for him. So he continued. Little did he know that writing down his experiences would recreate these experiences for millions of Christians in the following centuries as well. Ignatius' writings have come to be known as "The Spritual Exercises of Saint Ignatius Loyola."

Ignatius gave these spiritual exercises to many of his contemporaries in the form of individually-directed thirty day retreats. His purpose was to convert hearts to the desire for God, to love with the love of God, and to find God in all things.

Over the past fourteen years, I have given these same Spiritual Exercises of Saint Ignatius of Loyola, the thirty day individually-directed retreat, to many priests, sisters, religious, and lay men and women at the

Seal of the Society of Jesus

Jesuit Retreat House in Los Altos, California.

One may ask, what are these "Spiritual Exercises?" It is easy enough for us to identify with the word "exercise." We immediately think of the many various types of physical exercise there are.

There are physical exercises for every part of our bodies: legs, arms, back, neck, upper back, lower back, forearm, biceps, wrists, calf, lower leg, and on it goes.

In order to feel fit, we need to do physical exercise. If we do not, we feel lethargic. We lack the energy we need to feel good. It is the same spiritually. To feel fit, we need to do "spiritual exercises."

The Spiritual Exercises of Saint Ignatius Loyola are a series of meditations, contemplations, considerations, silent and spoken prayers, the examination of consciousness and other exercises that are "spiritual." All of these exercises are a means to nurture our desire for God, to love with God's love, and to find God in all things. Ignatius establishes a priority of importance among these various spiritual exercises. He establishes one exercise, the examination of consciousness, as being a must in our daily lives. Ignatius' overriding concern is to "see God in all things", to find God in the events and moments of our days. This seeking and finding, which today is called "discerning the presence of God" enables us to give our lives over to God's love. It is discerning the presence, the love, and the call of God in the experiences of our daily lives. It is the essence of the examination of consciousness, for it is an exercise in our seeking out God's active seeking out of us in the daily moments, events, and experiences of our lives. Ignatius instructs us to perform this prayer exercise twice a day, once at about noon and once before we go to bed, for a period of between ten and fifteen minutes each time. The examination of consciousness is quite simple in its dynamic. It has five basic dimensions: one, an act of the presence of God in thanksgiving; two, a prayer for the gift of being able to see God in every experience of our day; three, a reflective overview of our past hours; four, asking God for the gift of gratitude for His love and gifts and a healing sorrow for our own brokenness of response; and five, an overview of our immediate future hours with a renewed sensitivity to God's presence and call.

Here I would like to briefly comment on each of these aspects, beginning with an act of the presence of God in thanksgiving. In all prayer, we are to make an act of the presence of God as we begin. This act acknowledges that God at all times with us, sees us exactly as we are, and knows precisely what is in our hearts. This creates the same sense as a reading of Psalm 139.

Yahweh, you examine me and know me.
You know if I am standing or sitting.

This act of the presence of God should take no more than a minute. The knowledge that God knows every thought we think, every word we speak, and every detail of our conduct results in a sense of intimacy with God. This sense of intimacy is derived from the fact that the only One who could know so much about us must have created us, as we hear again from Psalm 139:

It was you who created my inmost self
and put me together in my mother's womb.
For all these mysteries I thank you.
For the wonder of myself.
For the wonder of your work.

The only response to this is THANK YOU! The only response is a gratitude and a joy at God's intimate love and concern for us as individuals, guiding us and holding us.

The act of the presence of God in thanksgiving is, without a doubt, a confidence builder. With God so close to us and so concerned for us, He shows us in a very inviting way how approachable he is. So in this atmosphere we can approach our loving God with a prayer, a prayer of petition. We can ask our God, in this second feature of the examination of consciousness, for the grace to see God in all things, in every aspect of our daily lives. Here we can ask our God for the ability to perceive His loving call to us in the events we have experienced and the people we have encountered. We ask for the grace of discernment, the discernment of God's spirit in our lives. We ask for the grace of a discerning heart, one that seeks and finds our beloved, God, in all things.

The third moment of the examination of consciousness is a reflective overview of the previous portion of the day. What has been happening to us? The focus here is on what the Lord has been doing in our lives over the past few hours. How is the Lord seeking us out? What is the gift that God is giving us? What is the Lord calling us to do? The first purpose, then, of this reflective overview of the last few hours of our day is to see God's action. The second purpose of this overview is to see our own reactions and actions.

This looking at our experiences of the past few hours needs to be an open and honest one, not one that dissects and analyzes the experiences away, but one that receives the experiences. This needs to be not an overview that excludes part of our experiences or controls our memories or feelings, but one that allows our experiences to speak the truth to us — one that allows the creator of our lives to speak to us.

So often we have heard, "Well it's easy to see that in hindsight" or "It's easy to be a Monday morning quarterback." What is being said here is that "in the heat of battle" or "when we are in the midst of something" it is often not so easy to see clearly all that is going on. But when the experience is over, the dust settles, and we look back on it with the help of grace, we can often see clearly what was going on. This is exactly the purpose of this reflective overview. As Socrates, the ancient Greek philosopher said, "the unexamined life is not worth living." The purpose here, then, is to reflectively look back over all that has gone on in the past few hours in order to clearly recognize God's call to us so that we can respond in a better, more loving, and deeper way.

In this exercise the grace we seek is to see God's presence, God's love, and God's call to us clearly. The grace we seek is to see our own giftedness and to see our own brokenness. As we receive this grace, we perceive God's loving action in our lives over the past few hours. We see our giftedness. We see the gifts God has given us. We also see our reaction, our gratitude, and our brokenness. We see our interfacing with God. Often what we see is that our responses to God's grace were not as good as they could be. If this is the truth, a healthy reaction occurs. This is the developing of a discerning heart. This is experiencing God's love for us as we come to joyfully and peacefully see who we are before our loving God. There is a growing sense here that we need God in order to love, to be loving, and to act in a loving manner. There is a growing sense in us that God is with us, showing us that we are sinners, but that God loves us dearly.

There is an obvious reaction that is normal to our seeing clearly the invitation of God in our lives. Our response often is, "Look at that, God's grace, and I did not see it, did not respond to it. I was not ready to seize the moment and love with God's love, love with the inspiration of God's grace." We react with some horror and dismay at the chasm between God's grace and our own responses. This sense of the inadequacy of our own responses results in a sense of sorrow that is healing, a sense of sorrow that is filled with grace, and a sense of sorrow that is joyful and hopeful. This is the fourth dimension of the examination of consciousness: to ask God for a sorrow that heals and for forgiveness. This gift of sorrow and forgiveness is surrounded by and comes from a sense of gratitude to God for God's invitation and promptings to us through our ordinary experiences of the last few hours.

As we look at and see our own failings and the evil

in our own lives, in a mysterious way we can be nourished if we acknowledge the truth about ourselves and offer that truth to God in prayer. It is here that we ask God to heal us of our wounds and sinfulness and to heal anyone that we have perhaps offended. This sense of need on our part comes from a grace-filled sense in us that we are often at the mercy of our own sinfulness except for the love and saving grace of Christ in our lives.

We now offer ourselves to our God. We offer to God the gifts we have received, as well as our sins, our weaknesses, and our lack of response. We offer to God all that we are, exactly as we are, in deed and in truth.

As the reflective overview of our ordinary experience over the last few hours comes to a close through the healing of God's grace, our natural tendency is to look with renewed vigor, hope, and anticipation toward the future. Saint Ignatius of Loyola uses these words for this fifth, and final, aspect of the examination of consciousness: "The fifth point will be to resolve to amend with the grace of God." As we look over the ordinary experiences of our morning, for example, and see God's love, God's grace, God's invitation to us and the inadequacy of our own responses, we become sensitized to this in a new and deeper way. Now in the fifth aspect of this prayer, we allow ourselves to look over our projected afternoon and evening experiences. We forecast, if you will, what will be our opportunities to love with God's grace. We look to be in deeper union with God's loving grace to us through our ordinary experiences. This is to create in us an ever deepening discerning heart. Our skill becomes sharper, keener, in flowing with the love of God in our lives, the prompting of the Holy Spirit of God in and through the ordinary experiences of our day. The more we do this, the more we will be able to trust the leading presence of God calling us to grow in love through these experiences. Can we see God here? This is an exercise. This prayer of examination of consciousness is an exercise. It is a workout. It is only by exercising that we will be fit, in shape, healthy … physically. The same is true spiritually. To be alive in love we need this spiritual exercise, this practical prayer of reflectively looking for God's presence in our ordinary experiences. We need this in order to have healthy, vigorous, sensitive lives with our God who is love. We are seeking the ability to love God with all our hearts, all our minds, and with all of our strength. We are seeking to love our brothers and sisters with the love of God. We are seeking to fulfill the command of our God and become who we have always wanted to be.

So to summarize, the spiritual exercise we need to

do to be spiritually fit is to examine our consciousness using, if you will, Saint Ignatius' five suggestions:

1. Make an act of the presence of God in thanks giving ... be aware that God sees you and knows you.

2. Pray for the gift of being able to see God in every experience of your day.

3. Make a reflective overview of the past few hours of your day.

4. Ask for the gift of gratitude for gifts received and for the gift of a sorrow that heals.

5. Look over the immediate future hours with a renewed sensitivity to God's presence and call to you.

Chapter Two
The Way, the Truth, and the Life

As we begin to apply the examination of consciousness to our daily experiences of love, of joy, of need, of fear, of sorrow, and of anger, I would like to consider that Jesus, the image of the God we have not seen, said of himself: "I am the way, the truth, and the life" (John 14:6). It is reasonable for us, then, to assume that if we go to Jesus, some aspect of the mystery of our own lives will be revealed to us. If we go to Jesus, some aspect of who we are now in our daily lives will be revealed to us. If we go to Jesus, some aspect of the mystery of the daily lives we live will become clear to us. We will see. We will understand. Why? Because God sent Jesus to us so that we could see who God is and so that we could see, understand, and know who we are and live our lives in the peace of God.

God sent Jesus to us to be our way, our truth, and our life and to show us how we could be who we have always wanted to be. If we look at Jesus, we will see how we will be fulfilled. If we look at Jesus, we will see how we will be free, because Jesus is given to us so that our joy may be complete.

What does Jesus mean to us? What does the life of Jesus mean to us? Jesus' words? Jesus' actions? Jesus' experiences? What does it mean that God experienced human life? What is Jesus saying to us about our daily human experiences by experiencing daily human life as one of us?

I think this can be found if we explore the answer to the question: 'What is holiness?" We find many answers to that question. We say "this person is holy" or "that person is holy." Ultimately, however, it is God who is in charge of what holiness means, not you and me. God is creator and Lord of all, even holiness and what holiness is. I would like to suggest that Jesus, the image of the God we have never seen, is the holiness of God. I would like to suggest that Jesus is the norm of holiness. What Jesus does is what holiness is. What Jesus says is what holiness is. What Jesus experienced is what holiness is, because Jesus is holiness. Jesus makes the definition of what holiness is because Jesus is in charge of all things. You and I do not make the definition of what holiness is. Jesus makes the meaning of all things, even the meaning of holiness.

Jesus found in his daily life experiences as one of us that to be himself, he had to allow his inner spirit, his self, to interact with his daily world around him. Jesus found that he had a choice, that he could express his inner reactions to his daily life experiences or he could repress these reactions to the world around him. Jesus realized that he continually evaluated the world around him by the norm of himself, by his own internal reactions. He could allow them to engage the daily world around him or he could repress, deny, and ignore them. Jesus chose to allow his emotional reactions to engage the daily world around him by expressing them in action.

What were his internal reactions to the world around him? They were love, joy, need, fear, sorrow, and anger. How did Jesus express these internal reactions? By holding, enjoying, trembling, crying, and calling out. Jesus realized that he was put in touch with who he was by living his reactions to the world in the world. This was holiness for Jesus. I believe this is 'holiness'' for us, also. Jesus is the way, the truth, and the life. It will be the same for us.

Here I would like to use the method of prayer, the spiritual exercise, we have just considered: the examination of consciousness. As we continue our journey into experiencing God, this prayer is a way of reflecting on our daily experiences of love, of joy, of need, of fear, of sorrow, and of anger.

Chapter Three
Experiences of Love

As we begin, let us look at ourselves. Do we as human beings experience and feel love? Do we express love? Is love a friend or a fearful foe of ours? Do we allow ourselves to experience the love we feel, or do we repress and deny this experience? Do we have an ensemble of love behaviors? Do we have ten love behavior "cassettes" that we can choose from to put into our behavior video cassette recorder so that we can express appropriately the feelings of love we have? Do we have ten love behavior floppy discs so that we can choose the appropriate one to put into our "behavior computer" in order to choose and match the appropriate love expressions to our feelings? Love has many expressions: offering a word of support, giving a helping hand, shopping for someone sick, spending time with a prisoner in jail, going out with a person on a date, listening to someone share a joyful experience, answering someone's question, untangling a kite string, carrying the lunch down to the beach, going back to the store for a forgotten item, spending the rest of our life with a spouse, for example.

Are we free to experience the love we feel for those around us? Are we free to express it? What is God saying to us through our experiences of love?

Let us look at the Lord. When was Jesus loving? Did Jesus ever feel love and express it? The answer can be found by looking at, contemplating, and praying over Jesus gathering the little children and holding them in his arms. The answer can be found in Jesus looking at the widow of Nain with great love, raising her son from the dead, and giving him back to her. Yes, Jesus felt love, and Jesus expressed it. This means that to feel love and to express love is "holy"-God-like, because Jesus our God felt love and expressed it.

People were bringing little children to him for him to touch them. The disciples turned them away, but when Jesus saw this he was indignant and said to them: "Let the little children come to me; do not stop them, for it is to such as these that the kingdom of God belongs. I tell you solemnly, anyone who does not welcome the kingdom of God like a little child will never enter it." Then he took them in his arms and blessed them, laying his hands upon them (Mark 10:13-16).

Now soon afterwards he went to a town called Nain, accompanied by his disciples and a great number of people. When he was near the gate of the town, it happened that a dead man was being carried out for burial, the only son of his mother, and she was a widow. And a considerable number of the townspeople were with her. When the Lord saw her his heart went out to her. "Do not cry,"

Village of Naim, Israel, where Jesus raised the widow's son.

he said. Then he went up and put his hand on the bier, and the bearers stood still, and he said, "Young man, I tell you to get up." The dead man sat up and began to talk, and Jesus gave him to his mother (Luke 7:11-16).

Are we free to feel love and to express love as Jesus did? Do we feel a call within us to do this, to live as Jesus lived? What is God saying to us through our daily life experiences of love? Let us allow God to move us! Allow God to illuminate and inspire us to choose the appropriate expressions of our feelings!

As we turn over in our hearts and minds these experiences of love, as we examine our consciousness, the grace of God meets us. God reveals his presence. God reveals the grace of perceiving God in all things. God shows Himself. God shows how close He is to us. God shows how He personally cares for us and how He loves us personally. This is a gift. This is grace. It is given to those who ask for it and who give God the opportunity to give it to them. And that is really what the examination of consciousness is — giving God the time and the opportunity to give us love and grace — to see God in all things.

As we look at ourselves in examining our consciousness, we take in our experiences of love. In doing so we are exposed to the many dimensions of these experiences. There are elements of self-centeredness, and there is the tender loving concern of God for us personally in the experience. We feel an intimate presence of God in the experience, and we feel a deep invitation from God to be more open and honest about who we are. We receive God's Word to us in our experience. All of this is prayer. It is experiencing God in our daily lives, our daily life experience of love. All of this is the gift of the Holy Spirit: wisdom, counsel, holiness, knowledge, perseverance, discernment and love. Our response is an opening to God, a turning to God in trust, and a surrendering to the leading and inviting hand of God. We give ourselves over to grace. We offer ourselves to our God by entering into our daily experiences of love. We offer ourselves to God through them, through prayerfully looking at our experiences, through receiving them, through giving ourselves over in response to the Word of God in them. This is prayer.

Let us allow our God to be close to us and reveal His presence to us. Let us look at our daily life experiences of love. Let us look at the daily life experiences of love of Christ our God. And let us enter prayerfully into this habit of reflecting.

Chapter Four
Experiences of Joy

As we begin, let's look at ourselves, at our own experiences of joy in our daily lives. As this habit of reflecting deepens, let us look at the joy we feel at a beautiful sunrise, the joy we feel as projects we have been working on are successful. We see the joy we feel at being alive as we walk through a forest, as we swim in a lake, as we cook wonderful meals, as we play the piano, as we hear the word of God preached, as we dance, as we listen to beautiful music, as we share with God in prayer... on and on. Our response is JOY! Our response is gratitude! Our response is joy in the gift received! We express this joy quite simply by ENJOYING. We express this joy by watching a beautiful sunrise, savoring success, by walking, swimming, cooking, playing the piano, dancing, listening to beautiful music.

What is your experience of joy? Do you feel joy? Are you joyful? Can you enjoy yourself? Can you enjoy others? Can you enjoy the gifts of God around you? What is God saying to you in and through your daily life experiences here?

Was Jesus joyful? When did Jesus ever feel the emotional reaction of joy and express it? In some ways this seems like an "un-holy" question or something irreverent to ask of our God. I think we feel this way from a notion that prayer is ethereal and quiet and that joy is loud and noisy. So, of course, joy is really not God-like or holy.

The answer to our question can be seen if we look at, contemplate, and pray over Jesus at the wedding feast at Cana.

Three days later there was a wedding at Cana in Galilee. The mother of Jesus was there, and Jesus and his disciples were invited. When they ran out of wine, the mother of Jesus said to him, "They have no wine."

Jesus said, "Woman, why turn to me? My hour has not come yet." His mother said to the servants, "Do whatever he tells you." There were six stone water jars standing there, meant for the ablutions that are customary among the Jews. Each could hold twenty or thirty gallons. Jesus said to the servants, "Fill the jars with water," and they filled them to the brim. 'Draw some out now," he told them, "and take it to the steward." They did this; the steward tasted the water, and it had turned into wine. Having no idea where it had come from — only the servants who had drawn the water knew — the steward called the bridegroom and said, "People generally serve the best wine first, and keep the cheaper sort till the guests have had plenty to drink, but you have kept the best wine till now." This was the first of

Wedding At Cana

the signs given by Jesus. It was given at Cana in Galilee. He let his glory be seen, and his disciples believed in him (John 2:1-11).

We know how joyful wedding feasts are. We also know from the Gospel writings of John that "there was a wedding feast at Cana in Galilee and Jesus and his disciples were invited." We know what it means to invite someone to a party. We want to invite people to our party who we know will enjoy themselves, have a good time, and help others enjoy themselves. Often people who cannot enjoy themselves are not invited because we know that they will not have a good time, and as a result, perhaps spoil the party. Jesus and his disciples were invited. This means that they knew Jesus could genuinely enjoy such festivities.

We also know that Jesus' first miracle was here when he changed the water in six stone water jars, each containing twenty gallons, into wine. One hundred and twenty gallons of wine...to keep the party going! We simply need to contemplate this scene for the answer.

Did Jesus feel joy? The answer is "YES!" This means that to feel joy and to enjoy is holy, God-like, because Jesus did this. This is so because what Jesus felt and did is what "holiness" is and what "holiness" means.

So let us look at ourselves now in our examination of consciousness. Let us explore our experiences of joy during the last hours. Let us see that they are the gift of God.

Do we see these experiences of joy as gifts from God? And did we enjoy these gifts, or did we pass them by? Let us see the call for union with the joyful Jesus. This joy is holy.

It is by reflecting on our experiences of joy in the examination of consciousness that we allow God the time and the opportunity to reveal to us His presence, His closeness, and His passionate love for us in and through our experiences of joy.

It is here that we experience how far we are from enjoying the real gifts God has for us in the world. It is here that we can perceive how we hunger for this joy. Let us accept God's gifts. Let us offer ourselves to our God in gratefulness by accepting and meeting God in them. Let us reflect on our own experiences of joy and on the experiences of joy of Christ our God. Let us enter prayerfully into this habit of reflecting.

Chapter Five
Experiences of Need

I would like to again begin by looking at our own human experiences. Do we as human beings have needs? Let us look at ourselves and see.

We human beings, men and women, need sleep, food, water, shelter, clothes, friends, love, warmth, schooling, exercise, a job, financial security, and prayer, just for starters!

I would like to focus on our needs for human relationships.

It is a hard won victory to be able to say "I need you" in today's society, because the phrase has in it a very real quality of "I am dependent on you."

The ideal of independence is so strongly prized in our society, that to be truly dependent on someone is looked upon as weakness. An example of this is that today if a woman says that she needs a man, her husband, she is looked upon as being un-liberated. For a man to say that he needs a woman, his wife, he is looked upon as weak, unmanly, or un-macho. This causes troubles in marriage and family life, because men and women need each other. Women and men depend on each other. Mutual need deepens the bonds of a relationship. Complementary gifts, talents, and needs serve as a basis for understanding and sharing. Saint Ignatius says in his "Contemplation to Attain Divine Love," which ends his Spiritual Exercises, that "love means that one shares what one has with one's beloved."

Ignatius says, "Love consists in a mutual sharing of goods; for example, the lover gives and shares with the beloved what he/she possesses, or something of that which he/she has or is able to give and vice versa. The beloved shares with the lover. So if one has knowledge, they share it with the one who do not possess it and so also with honors, riches, or anything else."

This sharing, then, can only be really given and received if we are comfortable with and familiar with the experience of need, of being needy. If we realize we are needy — for example, if a woman recognizes and accepts comfortably that she needs a man or if a man recognizes and accepts comfortably that he needs a woman — then we can ask another to meet our needs. As we are comfortable and familiar with our experiences of need, we can then recognize what is going on when another asks us to meet their need. We are in a position to recognize the naturalness and the goodness in this when we are asked to meet the need of another. We can then respond in a spirit of reciprocity and sharing and not in a spirit of resentment that we are being imposed upon.

It is appropriate for us to need each other. It is appropriate for us to need God, to need the love of God to live, and to need God's grace, comfort, wisdom, support, courage, and strength. This is acceptable. There is nothing wrong with us if we need God. As Saint Augustine so aptly put it, "Our hearts are made for you, O Lord, and they will not rest until they rest in you." So if we find ourselves needing God throughout our daily experiences, turning our hearts and minds to God in need, we should not worry! There is nothing wrong with us. We are God's children, and we need God's love in our lives to be who we are, to be who we have always wanted to be.

When our needs are filled, when our hunger for food is filled by bread, potatoes, meat, cheese, vegetables, fruit, and cake, it is a sign of God's love for us. When our needs for love are filled by parents, friends, spouses, and children loving us, it is God reaching into our days with gifts. When God invites us to come to him, it is a gift of love for us from God to fulfill us.

Do we accept our needs? Our neediness? Let us look at Jesus as we ask ourselves that question. Did Jesus ever have needs? Was Jesus ever needy? This may seem like an "un-holy" or disrespectful question, but I do not think it is. Simply look at, pray over, and contemplate the scene of Mary and Joseph with the newborn child Jesus in Bethlehem.

Now at this time Ceasar Augustus issued a decree for a census of the whole world to be taken. This was the first census that took place while Quirinius was governor of Syria, and everyone went to his own town to be registered. So Joseph set out from the town of Nazareth in Galilee and traveled up to Judea, to the town of David called Bethlehem, since he was of David's house and line, in order to be registered together with Mary, his betrothed, who was with child.

While they were there, the time came for her to have her child, and she gave birth to a son, her firstborn. She wrapped him in swaddling clothes and laid him in a manger, because there was no room for him in the inn. In the countryside close by there were shepherds who lived in the fields and watched their flocks during the night. The angel of the Lord appeared to them, and the glory of the Lord shone around them. They were terrified, but the angel said, "Do not be afraid. Listen, I bring you news of great joy, a joy to be shared by all the people. Today in the town of David a savior has been born to you; he is Christ the Lord. And here is a sign for you: you will find a baby

Christmas Night
The Star Over the Hills of Bethlehem

wrapped in swaddling clothes and lying in a
manger. And suddenly with the angel there was
a great throng of the heavenly host, praising God
and singing:

"Glory to God in the highest heaven,
and peace to all who enjoy his favor."

Now when the angels had gone from them into
heaven, the shepherds said to one another, "Let us
go to Bethehem and see this thing that has happened which the Lord has made known to us." So
they hurried away and found Mary and Joseph, and
the baby lying in the manger. When they saw the
child, they repeated what they had been told about
him, and everyone who heard it was astonished
at what the shepherds had to say. As for Mary, she
treasured all these things and pondered them in
her heart. And the shepherds went back glorify-
ing and praising God for all they had heard and
seen; it was exactly as they had been told
(Luke 2: 1-20).

Was Jesus, as a newborn baby, needy as we are
needy? Simply look at Jesus helpless. Simply contemplate and pray over Jesus needing to be fed, needing
to be clothed, needing to have his head held up so it
would not fall, needing to be taught how to walk, and
you will find the answer. Yes, Jesus was needy. Yes, Jesus
needed help. Jesus had a need for others. Yes, Jesus

asked others to meet his needs. This means that to be needy is "holy" because Jesus was needy, and Jesus is "holiness." This means that to ask another to meet our needs is "holy" because Jesus was needy and Jesus asked others to meet his needs. And Jesus is "holiness!" What Jesus did is the definition of what holiness is.

Are we aware of our own needs? Do we feel comfortable being needy? Do we know how to ask another to meet our own needs? Do we shut all of this off and repress this whole dynamic because we think this is weakness or because we do not want to owe anyone anything? Because we do not want to be indebted to anyone? Because we do not want to become dependent on anyone for anything? Maybe because the last time we trusted another to meet a need, we were disappointed and let down, and we do not want to be put in that position again. Maybe the last time we trusted another by sharing our need, it was used against us, and we were hurt deeply. So we are anxious about our own neediness.

As we become absorbed in our experiences of need during our examination of consciousness, we allow God the time to reveal His close presence and supporting love for us. God shares the gift of wisdom, counsel, and discernment for us to love and accept our own neediness in God's presence as Jesus did.

We are able to look at our own neediness honestly with a friend, Jesus, who was needy as we are and who had all of the needs that we have. Jesus invites us to become aware of our own needs, our own neediness, as he was aware of his. The grace of Christ calls us to trust, to take the step of asking another to meet our needs, to trust as we reveal to ourselves and others our own neediness. This is grace. Do we feel this call of God?

Let us offer ourselves to our God through our daily life experience of our own need by accepting our neediness as a gift, as a friend, as holy, as Jesus accepted his own neediness in becoming one of us. Let us reflect on our own experiences of need and the experiences of need of Jesus our God. Let us enter prayerfully into this habit of reflecting.

Chapter Six
Experiences of Fear

Do we human beings ever experience fear? Let's look at ourselves!

We human beings experience fear of war, fear of heights, fear of wild animals, fear of earthquakes, fear of driving, fear of violent weather, fear of being attacked, fear of being raped, fear of being robbed, fear of being harmed, and the list goes on and on.

Fear is a human feeling that can paralyze us. We often hear that someone was "frozen with fear." Fear can have this effect on us in a variety of circumstances because we do not know what we are feeling. We do not know that we are afraid, and we do not know what it is that we fear. It is the anxiety or embarrassment created by not knowing what is going on that results in our being 'frozen" or "paralyzed."

It is only by being able, bit by bit, to become aware that we are afraid, then become aware of what exactly it is that we fear that we can prevent the anxiety and embarrassment level from paralyzing us.

This happens as we see that our fear is normal or that we need not be afraid of various people or experiences. In either of these realizations we begin to make friends with our fear. We stop treating our fear with disdain and contempt, and we begin to admire our fear and treat it with a sense of friendship. As we do this, our paralysis disappears and we are able to "be afraid" in peace. We treat fear as it should be treated: as a God-given gift for preserving our own safety, health, and valuable lives, as well as that of others, in the Lord.

Are we often paralyzed or frozen by fear in a way that we can repress the entire experience? Is fear our friend or foe? Is fear a familiar experience for us? What is God saying to us about our experiences of fear?

Did Jesus ever feel fear and tremble? Was Jesus ever afraid? Again, are such questions disrespectful? I do not think so. Simply pray over, contemplate, and see Jesus in the garden of Gethsemane. He poured out sweat in fear as he shook and trembled at the possibility of being crucified.

They came to a small estate called Gethsemane, and Jesus said to his disciples, "Stay here while I pray." Then he took Peter, James, and John with him. And a sudden fear came over him and great distress. And he said to them, "My soul is sorrowful to the point of death. Wait here and keep awake" (Mark 14:32-34).

Then he withdrew from them, about a stone's

Olive Tree in the Garden

throw away, and knelt down and prayed. "Father," he said, "if you are willing, take this cup away from me, nevertheless let your will be done, not mine." Then an angel appeared to him, coming from heaven to give him strength. In his anguish he prayed even more earnestly, and his sweat fell to the ground like great drops of blood (Luke 22: 41-44).

He came back to the disciples and found them sleeping, and he said to Peter, "So you had not the strength to keep awake with me one hour? You should be awake and pray not to be put to the test. The spirit is willing, but the flesh is weak." Again, a second time, he went away and prayed, "My Father," he said, "if this cup cannot pass by without my drinking it, your will be done!" And he came back again and found them sleeping, their eyes were so heavy. Leaving them there, he went away again and prayed for the third time, repeating the same words. Then he came back to the disciples and said to them, "You can sleep on now and take your rest. Now the hour has come when the Son of Man is to be betrayed into the hands of sinners (Matthew 26: 40-45).

This means that to be afraid, to feel fear and to shake and tremble is "holy" because Jesus was afraid, Jesus felt fear, Jesus shook, and Jesus trembled. And Jesus is "holiness." What Jesus experienced is holy.

This can allow us to bring in our experiences of fear in our daily lives through our examination of consciousness. We can bring these experiences in as friends, as rich resources of God's giftedness to us, rather than filter fearful experiences out. Let us allow God to speak to us through our fear of our union with God. This is the same fear that Jesus experienced.

As we look over our experiences of fear in this examination of consciousness, the presence of God conforting us with his strength is given. God's desire is to show himself to us. The constant call for us to "Turn your hearts to God" does not go unheard and unrewarded as God says again to us: "I will be with you all days even to the end of the world" (Matthew 28:20).

As we face our fearful experiences in examining our consciousness, we view them with our God who was afraid and trembled as we do. We have a friend. Here our dependence on the strength and wisdom of God who loves us results in our turning to God. He slowly nudges and supports us through frightening events and situations as a shepherd guides the sheep. God clarifies our vision so we can see what it is we fear. God's presence as a light in the darkness illuminates our way with wisdom, knowledge, and insight, enabling us to know how to proceed.

We find someone we can trust, someone who will guide us to shore safely. We can open ourselves to this guide, this light, this shepherd: Jesus the Lord. We can offer these experiences to our God. We form a bond, a bond that will last. Trust. Friendship. Unity. Love. Love that has been proven true by its ability to deal with the real experiences of our lives! So let us reflect on our own experiences of fear and the experiences of fear of Jesus our God. Let us enter prayerfully into this habit of reflecting.

Chapter Seven
Experiences of Sorrow

Is sorrow an experience for us human beings? Let us look at ourselves and see! When a loved one dies — our spouse, a parent, a child, a friend — we experience sorrow. When we lose a job, feel we have been betrayed, or are sorely disappointed, we experience sorrow. These are all losses. And losses evoke sorrow.

Sorrow is a deep, human, emotional reaction to a real or a perceived loss. Sorrow is a human, emotional reaction to the loss of a human relationship. When someone leaves or someone dies, it hurts. And hurt is an old-fashioned word for a combination of sorrow and anger at the one who is leaving or changing the relationship. This is painful. Sorrow is painful. It is the result of lost closeness.

Depression sets in. Darkness. Gloom. This is a common, everyday part of life. "Good-bye" is as much a part of life as "hello." Separation and the sorrow, pain, hurt, and anger that accompany it, are as much a part of life as union. Where and when there is closeness, there is also the potential for separation. The only way to avoid sorrow is to remain distant from everyone and everything, to love nothing. And even this is really no way to avoid sorrow, because it creates its own void and pain. The isolation and emptiness that result from loving nothing creates their own pain, and it is worse than any sorrow.

Was Jesus ever sorrowful? Did Jesus ever experience sorrow? Did Jesus ever cry? Are these questions proper? Jesus says, "Yes, they are!" as we contemplate, pray over, and see Jesus crying over Jerusalem.

As he drew near and came in sight of the city, he cried and shed tears over it and said, "If you in your turn had only understood on this day the message of peace! But, alas, it is hidden from your eyes! Yes, a time is coming when your enemies will raise fortifications all around you, when they shall encircle you and hem you in on every side" (Luke 19: 41-43).

Let us also contemplate, pray over, and see Jesus crying over Lazarus.

Mary went to Jesus, and as soon as she saw him, she threw herself at his feet, saying, "Lord, if you had been here, my brother would not have died." At the sight of her tears, and those of the Jews who followed her, Jesus said in great sorrow, with a sigh that came straight from the heart, "Where have you put him?" They said, "Lord, come and see." Jesus wept, and the Jews said, "See how much he loved him!" But there were some who remarked, "He opened the eyes of the blind man, could he not have prevented this man's death?" Still sighing, Jesus reached the tomb. It was a cave with a stone

Lazarus-The Tomb

to close the opening. Jesus said, "Take the stone away!" Martha said to him, "Lord, by now he will smell; this is the fourth day." Jesus replied, " Have I not told you that if you believe, you will see the glory of God?" So they took away the stone. Then Jesus lifted up his eyes and said: "Father, I thank you for hearing my prayer. I knew indeed that you always hear me when I speak for the sake of all these who stand around me, so that they may believe it was you who sent me."
When he said this, he cried in a loud voice, "Lazarus, here! Come out!" The dead man came out, his feet and hands bound with bands of linen and cloth round his face. Jesus said to them, "Unbind him, let him go free" (John 11:32-44).

This means that to feel sorrow and to cry is "holy" because Jesus felt sorrow and Jesus cried. And what Jesus experienced is "holy." What Jesus experiences is holiness.

In our examination of consciousness, let us bring in the loss and the sorrow we have experienced in the last hours. Let us see how Christ experienced this same sorrow. Let us see our deep union with Christ the Lord.

Experiencing anew our sorrow as we examine our consciousness in the presence of God allows the intimate closeness of God's nurturing care to be with us. We hold our grief to our God and feel God's understanding, God's union with us, Emmanuel, God with us. As we share our sorrow, we experience the presense of a friend, our creator and Lord. This is experiencing God in our daily life, our daily experience of sorrow. Let us contemplate the suffering, the sorrow, and the sense of loss that Jesus experienced. As we do this, we know that he understands what we are talking about when we bring our own experiences of sorrow, of separation, and of loss to him in our examination of consciousness. In this dialogue, this sharing with Christ, we receive the gift of seeing that our own suffering, our own sorrow, is the very same as Christ's. This is one event: Christ's sorrow and our sorrow. We feel the same pain. This grace results in a deep sense of our union with Jesus in our daily life experiences of sorrow. It is this union that brings meaning and peace. Let us reflect, then, on our own experiences of sorrow and the experiences of sorrow of Jesus our God. Let us enter prayerfully into this habit of reflection.

Chapter Eight
Experiences of Anger

Let us look at ourselves as we begin. Do we ever get angry? Somehow, this is a very controversial question. As human beings, we seem to answer this question with two totally opposite responses and feel quite justified in denying each alternative. For example, we say, "Sure, of course I get angry. Everyone gets angry." Or we can admit none of it and say, "I am a loving, faith-filled person. I am not an angry person, and I would not stoop so low." Actually, we have no real choice. Feelings are simply a reaction we have. As Saint Thomas Aquinas said, "Feelings are simply a response." Feelings are neither right nor wrong. They simply "are." And they "are" before we have a choice about them.

Someone scratches the paint on my brand-new car as it is parked in front of the supermarket. I come out and see it, and I get angry. Someone is supposed to bring a vegetable dish and the dessert to a pot-luck lunch, but they forget. I get angry. Someone comes up to me in the school yard and takes my lunch from me. I get angry.

A human being simply reacts, and a human being simply reacts with anger at being harmed. Anger is neither right nor wrong, it is simply a reaction. If anything, anger is good, a God-given reaction. Anger has done much good in the world as love has. How many tunnels have been dug because human beings were angry about having to climb over a mountain? Anger must be used constructively, rather than denied.

The anger human beings have about continually climbing over a mountain is to be used, not denied. Rather than repressing the anger, we need to allow our anger, our frustration, and our rage to move us to work to find a better way to get to the other side of the mountain. Eventually, our anger, frustration, and rage result in the dawning of the idea of tunneling through the mountain so that we will not have to climb over it again. But what work it takes to dig the tunnel! Where will we get the energy and strength to do such a job? We will get it from our anger, frustration, and rage, the God-given gift of human energy to change things that need to be changed.

Do we see our anger as our friend? If we do, do we have an ensemble of behavior actions to choose from that will appropriately express our feelings of anger?

Was Jesus ever angry? Did Jesus ever feel anger? And when did Jesus ever express anger? These also may seem like un-holy questions. But if we watch, contemplate, and pray over Jesus raising his voice at the Pharisees, calling them hypocrites, or if we watch Jesus taking a whip and driving the money changers out of the temple, we can see the answers to the questions.

> Alas for you, scribes and Pharisees, you hypocrites! You shut up the kingdom of heaven in men's and women's faces, neither going in yourselves nor allowing others to go in who want to. Alas for you, scribes and Pharisees, you hypocrites! You pay the tithe of mint, dill, and cummin and have neglected the weightier matters of the law — justice, mercy, good faith! These you should have practiced, without neglecting the others. You blind guides! Straining out gnats and swallowing camels!

> Alas for you scribes and Pharisees, you hypocrites! You clean the outside of the cup and dish and leave the inside full of extortion and imperfections. Blind Pharisees! Alas for you, scribes and Pharisees, you hypocrites! You are like whitewashed tombs that look handsome on the outside, but inside are full of dead men's bones and every kind of corruption. In the same way you appear to people from the outside, like good honest men, but inside you are full of hypocrisy and lawlessness. Serpents, brood of vipers, how can you escape being condemned to hell.
> (Matthew: 23:13,23-24,27- 28,33)

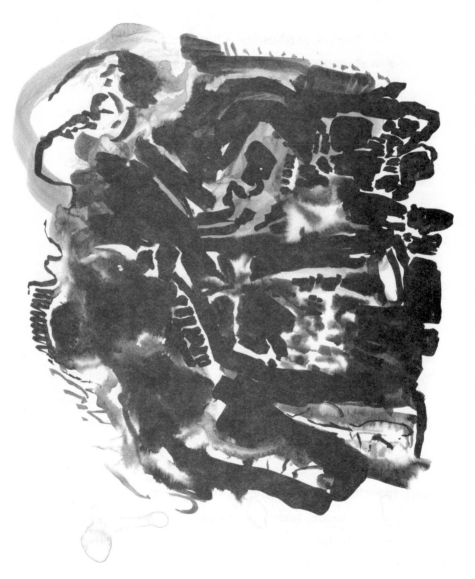

Anger

Just before the Jewish Passover, Jesus went up to Jerusalem. In the temple he found people selling cattle, sheep, and pigeons, and the money changers sitting at their counters there. Making a whip out of some cord, he drove them all out of the temple, cattle and sheep as well, scattered the money changers' coins, knocked their tables over, and said to the pigeon sellers, "Take all of this out of here and stop turning my Father's house into a market." Then his disciples remembered the words of Scripture: "Zeal for your house will devour me." The Jews intervened and said, "What sign can you show us to justify what you have done?" Jesus answered, "Destroy this sanctuary, and in three days I will raise it up." The Jews replied, "It has taken forty-six years to build this sanctuary. Are you going to raise it up in three days?" But he was speaking of the sanctuary of his body, and when Jesus rose from the dead, his disciples remembered that he had said this, and they believed the Scripture and the words he had said (John: 2: 13-22).

Yes, Jesus became angry! Very angry! And often! This makes becoming angry "holy" because Jesus is the holiness of God and what Jesus experienced is the very meaning of holiness.

This means that to be angry, to feel anger, and to express it is holy because Jesus felt anger, Jesus was angry, and Jesus expressed it. Let us allow the Lord to move us and to illuminate and inspire us to choose the appropriate expressions of our feelings of anger.

The question is, do we see our own anger as "holy?" We need to bring our experiences of anger over the last few hours into our examination of consciousness and hold them up to the lived experience of Jesus, allowing the grace of God to reveal God's presence here.

In looking at our experiences of anger in the context of prayer, in our examination of consciousness, the love of God allows us to accept our pain and accept our anger. God proves himself to be present instructing, illuminating, giving the gifts of perseverance, of justice, of courage, of strength, and of acceptance. Again, we allow a deep invitation from God in the experience to call us to be more open and honest about who we are. We receive God's Word in our experiences of anger. We again experience the many aspects of this feeling: dimensions of our own selfishness, the presence of God calling us closer to him, the call for us to be closer to ourselves and accept our own daily life experiences of anger as the Lord accepted and loved his own anger.

Here with Christ we look at our own anger. Here with Christ who was justly angry do we look with understanding upon our own experiences of anger. Here in our examination of consciousness, the grace of God can illuminate our just and holy anger. The grace of God can help us to acknowledge our anger as good, as a gift. Here the grace of God can illuminate us to know and choose the appropriate behavior and manner of expressing our anger.

Let us reflect on our own experiences of anger over the last few hours and on the experiences of anger in the daily life of Jesus our God. Let us enter into this prayer, the examination of consciousness, this habit of reflecting.

Chapter Nine
In Conclusion

In prayer we look at our daily life experiences. We experience in our daily lives the same love, joy, need, fear, sorrow, and anger as Jesus did. And since this is so, our daily life experience is holy. The working out of our daily reactions of love, joy, need, fear, sorrow, and anger and their appropriate expressions is really prayer. Seeking to live as Jesus lived, seeking the will of God, seeking God who is seeking us out in our daily life experiences, seeking to see God in all things. This is really prayer.

In order to see, we need to look every day. To exercise this capability of looking for God, seeking God in all things, seeking God who is seeking us in our daily life experiences, we need to examine our daily life experiences. We need to examine our consciousness. We need to develop a habit of reflecting. As we do this, we realize that all is a gift from God. As we come to know ourselves through examining our consciousness and our daily life experiences, we see everything we have as a gift from God. In our giftedness we come to know that all our talents, our health, our feelings of love, joy, need, fear, sorrow and anger, all cry out to us of God. If we believe that we earn the love of a friend, that loving with the love of God is the result of our careful efforts, that our personal holiness comes from our skills in managing our lives, or that growth in trust comes through our cleverness, we are naive and superficial. In this prayer we realize that all of life is God's gift to us, even our radical flaws.

In this daily "spiritual exercise" of realizing that God knows every detail of our lives, of asking for the gift of seeing God in our daily life experiences, of looking over the experiences of the last few hours, of asking for a gratefulness for gifts received and a sorrow that heals, and of looking over the next hours of our life, the five aspects of the examination of our life, the five aspects of the examination of consciousness, we become "spiritually fit." We receive the grace to indeed see, feel, and perceive the grace of God in our hearts, our minds, and in our very being. We are able to perceive God's presence in our lives. This is a gift. This taking time out to seek God is rewarded by finding God:

"Seek and you shall find, knock and it shall be opened to you, ask and you shall receive" (Luke: 11:9).

This simple stopping and praying, this simple "spiritual exercise," this "asking" twice a day results in the gift of seeing God in all things, of finding God, of receiving God in our daily lives, and of having discerning hearts. It is a grace which is in season at all times. The grace is endless, and it is everlasting. It will be poured upon us, pressed down and overflowing until we can love with the love of God that seeks us and everyone out, until we can live our daily lives as God's love and grace invites and prompts us.

The grace of this prayer exercise is to see that Jesus continues to live his life of love, joy, need, fear, sorrow, and anger in our own love, joy, need, fear, sorrow, and anger. The grace of this exercise prayer is to allow the Lord to move, illuminate, and inspire us to choose the appropriate expressions of our feeling experiences. The grace of this prayer exercise, this "spiritual exercise," is to see the many gifts we have received, that God has shared what He has with us, that God breathes life into all of this for us, that God labors in everything for us to bring us to love with God's love, the crowning fulfillment of our being, bringing us to who we've always wanted to be.

If God has given us so much in and through our daily life experiences, how do we respond? How do we return love? How do we bring all of these gifts in love back to God as gift? By offering ourselves, our lives, and the concrete details of our daily life experiences of love, joy, need, fear, sorrow, and anger back to God! We offer ourselves back to God through our daily life experiences by accepting them, loving them, living them and raising them to God in thanksgiving, that we might be the love of God in the world.

Published Books
by
Robert Fabing, S.J.

The Eucharist of Jesus:
A Spirituality For Eucharistic Celebration

Audio and Video Tape also available through
Epoch Universal Publications

Experiencing God in Daily Life

Audio Tape also available
Epoch Universal Publications

Published Collections
of
Liturgical Music
by
Robert Fabing, S.J.

* * *

Indwelling

Be Like the Sun

Song of the Lamb

Winter Risen

Everlasting Covenant

Epoch Universal Publications
10802 N. 23rd Ave
Phoenix, AZ 85029
1 (602)-864-1980

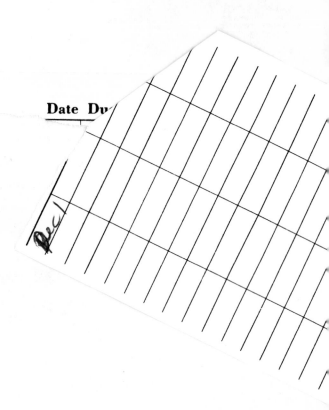

Date Dv